Fantastic Covers

And How to Make Them

Fantastic Covers

And How to Make Them

So, You Want to Write series
~Book 2~

THERESA SNEED

DEDICATION

Fantastic Covers and How to Make Them is dedicated to you. If you want to do anything worthwhile in life, then you must be willing to work hard and never give up. Writing is a skill that has to be developed and so is creating that perfect cover. As an author, I am continuously learning my craft, and you can too.

ACKNOWLEDGMENTS

The one group I have to acknowledge above all others is the writing group I belong to—American Night Writers Association. Without them, I would not be where I am today, or where I will be tomorrow. Thanks, ANWA.

Dear Reader,

I hope you enjoy reading *Fantastic Covers and How to Make Them.* If you loved this book, please consider leaving a good review everywhere—including my website. Your kind words might be the reason that someone else decides to read my books, and for that, I thank you in advance. ☺

Stay connected with new releases and free eBook offers by signing up at my website at www.theresasneed.com

- Author, Theresa Sneed

Other Titles by Theresa Sneed

No Angel Series
Angel with an Attitude
Earthbound Angel
Destiny's Angel
Earth Angel
Harold Angel Sing

Sons of Elderberry Series
Elias of Elderberry
The Wood Fairies of Estraelia
Missing Medallion

Escape Series
Escape
You Can't Hide
Find Her Keep Her

Salem Witch Haunt series
Salem Witch Haunt
Return to Salem
Salem Bewitched
Stranger Than Fiction

Brown Nose Bear

Facing Mortality
Dreams & Other Significant Things

So, You Want to Write
A Guide to Writing Your First Book

One

Yes, Judge a Book by Its Cover

What makes a fantastic cover? For me, it must be aesthetically pleasing to the eye. It must draw me in and capture my attention. While it does seem fickle to judge a book by its cover, we all do. So, the first thing one must do when creating a fantastic cover—is to study other book covers.

You can do this in one of two ways—go to bookstores and peruse your genre's book shelves and/or go to amazon.com best seller books. On the left hand side of amazon best sellers there is a list of book genres. Pick the one that most closely matches your genre and study the first ten to twenty (or more) book covers and then the last ten to twenty book covers in the top 100. Researching the top selling books in your genre can give you an idea of what works and what doesn't work.

Your book cover should represent the essence of your awesome story—or the incredible content of your book, if nonfiction. The reader's interest should be piqued, not only by the images on your cover, but also by the title.

I remember seeing a book recently whose title grabbed me right away, but the cover art work was so out of sync with the title, that I immediately judged the writing to be as juvenile as the art. Seems small minded doesn't it? But as much as I love reading, I have to choose the books I read carefully. There's nothing worse than investing time in a book just to find out it really wasn't worth my time.

Now, before you judge me as a book snob, let me tell you that not liking a book has little to nothing to do with not admiring the author for the tremendous effort they put into creating their book. Nor does it have anything to do with how wonderful I'm sure they are—it just means that if I feel that guarded about picking up poorly designed books with unattractive covers, there probably are hundreds just like me. And you really want a potential reader to get past your cover and into your great work.

TWO

What You Can Do, Might Surprise You

Creating a fantastic cover is something you can easily pay someone else to do, or you can do it yourself. I taught myself how to make covers. I use a free program called GIMP which you can download from the internet. Then I set about learning how to use the program by watching YouTube videos on specific topics.

Before you dive into GIMP and begin creating your fantastic cover, the first thing you have to do is have a book written—or at least partially written.

I'm a bit nontraditional in writing a manuscript. Most authors will wait until their novel is finished and then begin to format it, or they will pay someone else to format it. I format my books as I write. I taught myself how to and then kept copious notes which I later turned into a book called, "So, You Want to Write, A Guide to Writing Your First Book."

I usually write at least two chapters before I begin formatting, and then I format it and turn it into a book form. I like writing into the book form better than into an 8x11 manuscript. In fact, it is what I am doing right now.

If your book is already formatted, skip this next part and go straight to chapter three.

So, you have your book written, and you're ready to create the cover. You have to format it first, because in order to create the correct size cover, you have to know the dimensions of your book and the approximate book length for the thickness of the spine. Divide your manuscript into chapters and give each chapter a name or just a number. Use "Header 1" in the menu bar above your manuscript and modify it to meet your needs. Every time you create a new chapter, click on that "Header 1" or whatever you may have renamed it.

As I mentioned earlier, I am a little nontraditional in my approach, because I format my books as I write them, but you can follow these steps with your completed manuscript as well. After I have written a chapter or two, I take my 8x11 double-spaced manuscript and follow these steps:

1. Your manuscript should be set at Times New Roman 12.

If there aren't any special fonts in your manuscript, then highlight all text in your manuscript by pressing Ctrl + A, and then set the font at Times New Roman 12. If you do have special fonts for certain things, just do it one section at a time, but all of your manuscript minus special sections should be in Times New Roman 12 font.

2. Set the "space between lines" at 1.15.

To do this, hold down CTRL + A to highlight all text and then go to "Paragraph" in the hanging menu and click on the icon with the arrow going up and down "line and paragraph spacing" then set it to 1.15.

3. Justify manuscript.

Hold down CTRL + A, and then in the "Paragraph" box in the hanging menu, click on the "justified" icon, which is three lines of equal length stacked on top of each other.

4. Create front matter.

Front matter consists of the "title page", "other titles", "dedication page", "acknowledgments page", and etc. and are placed in the front of your book. There are examples of these later in this chapter.

5. Create back matter.

Back matter is placed in the back of your book and is your author bio and information pages. There are examples of these later in this chapter.

6. Resize manuscript.

I resize my manuscript from 8x11 to my desired book size of 5.5" x 8.5". Yours may be different, but I try to keep my books, regardless of genre, all the same size so they fit nicely on a bookshelf together. This is done by going to Page Layout, Size, More Paper Sizes, and then adjusting width to 5.5" and the height to 8.5". You'll notice that the paper size changed from "letter" to "custom" at that point.

7. Margins

I used CreateSpace (now just called KDP) for creating my books, so I go there to get the specific margin sizes for the length of my book. As I have only written a few chapters, I approximate what the length of the book will be and later adjust the margins to fit the actual number of pages written.

CreateSpace (KDP) is a free program unless you hire their professionals to do the work. Go to www.kdp.amazon.com and register if you aren't already using them. After you register, sign in. Use the search site in the upper right-hand corner and type in "book templates," and then click on "book interior guidelines."

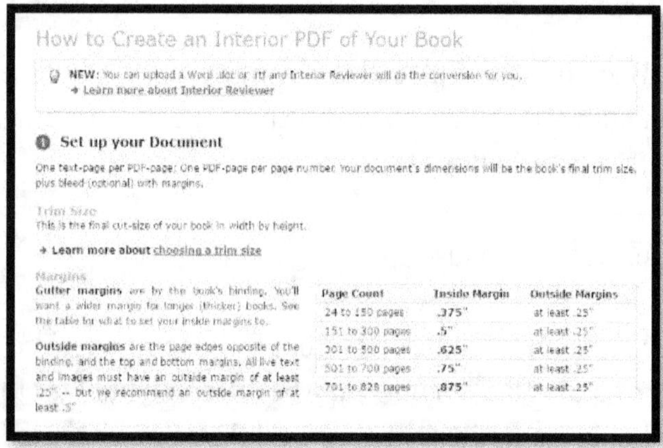

How to Create an Interior PDF of Your Book

NEW: You can upload a Word .doc or .rtf and Interior Reviewer will do the conversion for you.
→ Learn more about Interior Reviewer

Set up your Document

One text-page per PDF-page; One PDF-page per page number. Your document's dimensions will be the book's final trim size, plus bleed (optional) with margins.

Trim Size
This is the final cut-size of your book in width by height.

→ **Learn more about** choosing a trim size

Margins
Gutter margins are by the book's binding. You'll want a wider margin for longer (thicker) books. See the table for what to set your inside margins to.

Outside margins are the page edges opposite of the binding, and the top and bottom margins. All live text and images must have an outside margin of at least .25" -- but we recommend an outside margin of at least .5"

Page Count	Inside Margin	Outside Margins
24 to 150 pages	.375"	at least .25"
151 to 300 pages	.5"	at least .25"
301 to 500 pages	.625"	at least .25"
501 to 700 pages	.75"	at least .25"
701 to 828 pages	.875"	at least .25"

From this chart, you can see that if your book is 350 pages long (including front and back matter) the inside margin will be .625" and the outside margin will be at least .25". KDP recommends at least .5", so that is what I always set my outside margins at. Once you determine the margin size, go to your manuscript, and then go to Page Layout,

Margins, Custom Margins, and then adjust the margins to fit the requirements found on the chart per the length of your book. Make sure Apply to: is set on Whole document.

8. Create chapter headings, including chapter titles (in a finished manuscript this is easier to do as you create section breaks.)

To do this: type "Chapter One" at the top of your first chapter. Then under HOME right click on "Heading 1" from the menu. Choose "Modify" and then change the font, font size, color, etc. Now every time you add a new chapter heading, simply click on "Heading 1", which will have retained your settings for that type of heading.

Not all books have titles for their chapters, but mine do. Follow the same steps for adding the title of each chapter. Create your title, click on "Heading 2", and modify it to your wishes. Now each time you create a chapter title, click on "Heading 2" and it will assume those settings.

9. Section breaks between chapters.

Section breaks are usually done after you have a completed novel ready to format, but as I said earlier, my method is a bit nontraditional in that I format as I write my books. Once you have sized your book and given it the correct margins based on the number of pages in your book, the next step is creating section breaks between your front matter (title page, dedication page, acknowledgments page, etc.) and each one of your chapters. Your front matter will become section one, your first chapter will become section two, your second chapter will become section three, and so forth.

Here are the steps -

Step 1: Create your **front matter**.

There are two formulas I follow for this depending if my book is the first in a new series or the second or so in a continuing series.

This is the order of your front matter for a *new* series:

1. Title page (just the name of the title)

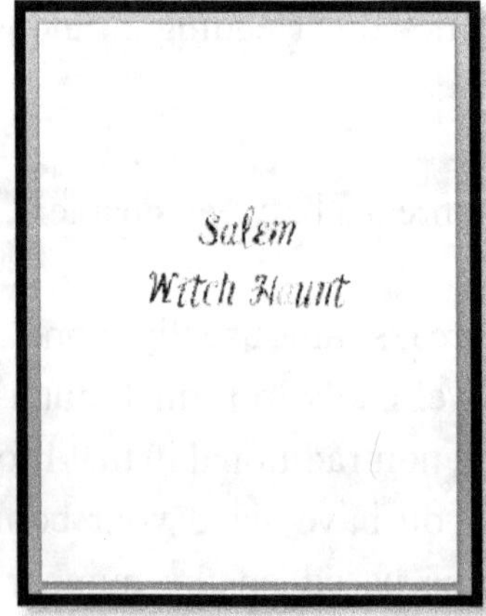

2. Blank page or "Other titles" if this is your second or third book, etc.

3. Title page/Author name

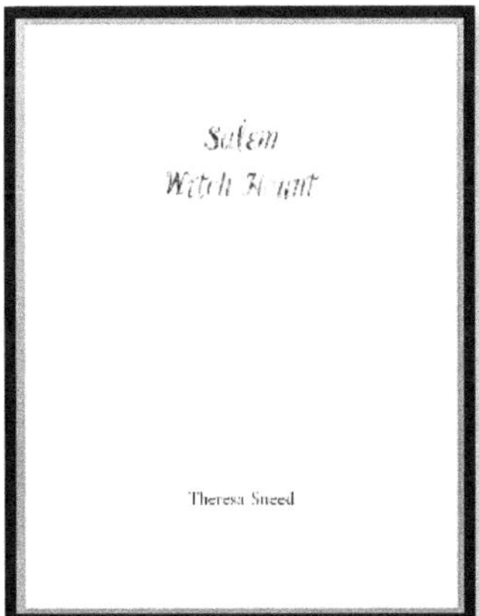

4. Dedication page. You can see that I added the copyright and ISBN here, but since then, I have moved those to the acknowledgments page.

5. Acknowledgments page

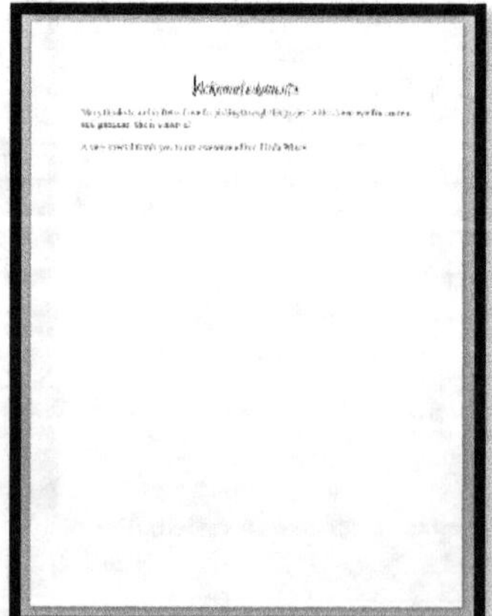

6. Blank page

7. Prologue page if you have one, if not skip steps seven and eight.

8. Blank page

This is what I follow for my front matter for a *continuing* series:

1. Praise for that series page - where you pull together endorsements from happy readers.
2. Praise for that series page (continued)
3. Title page with all volumes listed
4. Blank page
5. Title page (no author name here)
6. Blank page
7. Title page with author name
8. Dedication page
9. Acknowledgments page
10. Blank page
11. Prologue if you have one, otherwise skip 11 and 12
12. Blank page

Great! Now that you have your front matter ready, you can begin creating sections breaks.

SECTION BREAKS

1. You will first create a section break between your front matter and chapter one. To do this, pull the chapter heading for chapter one, along with the text, right next to

the last word (including punctuation marks) on the previous page (the last page in your front matter.)

Here is an image of my acknowledgment page (the last page of my front matter) right beside my chapter one.

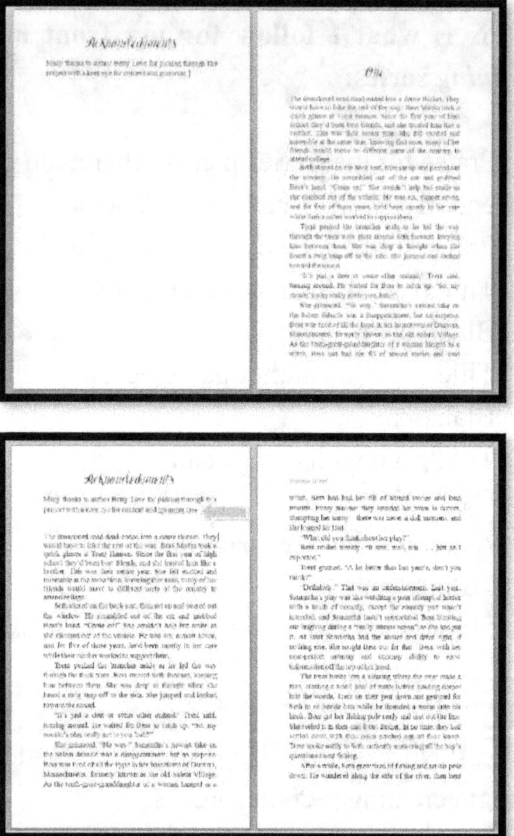

I pulled chapter "one" over to the acknowledgment page. You'll note that the chapter heading reduced to the regular font. I will change that back in the next few steps.

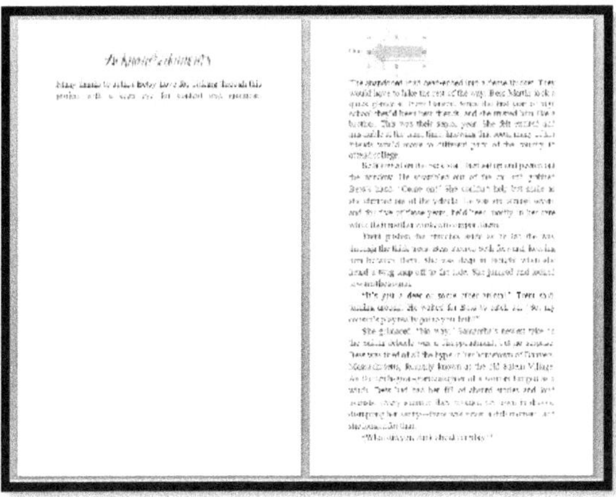

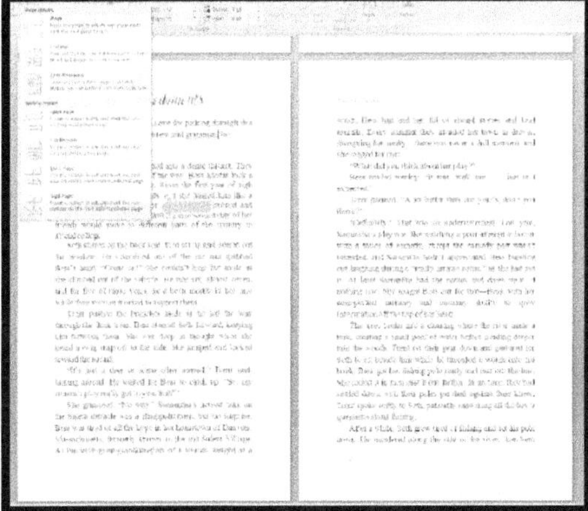

2. Now with your cursor right where you left it (in front of the word chapter, or "one" in my case) click on Page layout, Breaks, Odd page.

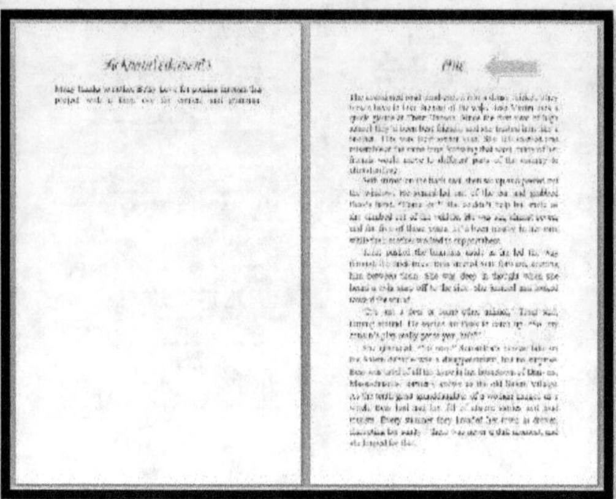

The image above shows what happens when you do step two. Once you click on "odd page" it will send your "chapter one" right back to where it was, as shown in the picture. You will note that "one" is now tiny and has lost its header status. You should have previously created a "Header 1" file that you used for each chapter and saved it in the menu bar above your manuscript. Simply click on the saved "Header 1" or whatever you might have named it, and your header will revert back to the settings you already saved for your book as shown in the next image.

The image above shows that after clicking on your saved header, your chapter header will revert back to the desired format previously saved.

Now you have created two sections. You can see this if your place your cursor in the far left or right corner (upper or lower) pulling up the headers and footers. It's hard to read, but it says "section 1" and "section 2" in the above picture.

3. You have to follow these steps at the end of each chapter, creating a new section with each chapter. Pull the next chapter right up to the last punctuation mark in the proceeding chapter and follow the same directions as you did above.

4. You've created section breaks for all your chapters and now you have to add the **back matter** which is the author bio and any information pages you have.

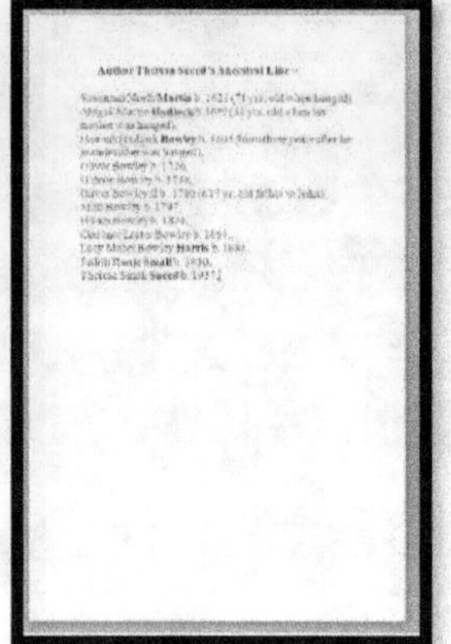 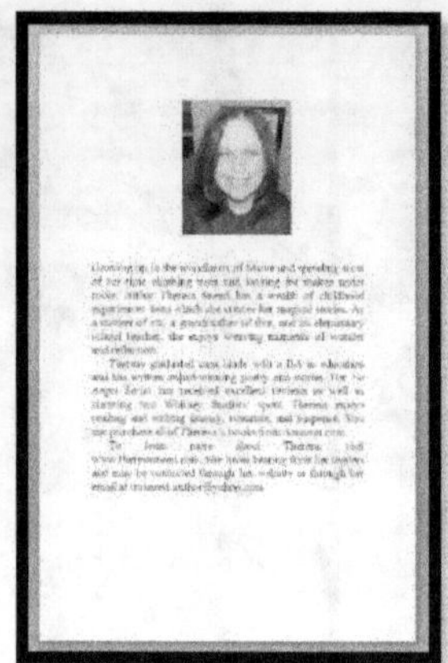

I added a genealogy page to show my direct link to one of the women hanged as a witch in Salem. (I am the 9th great granddaughter of Susannah North Martin.) Do a section break between the author bio including any information pages and the *last* word in your *last* chapter (including punctuation) just like you did for all the other section breaks.

5. Placing page numbers, author name, and title name in the interior of your book can seem impossible, but if you keep trying, you'll become a pro!

1. ONLY after section breaks are in place, click on the bottom left-hand corner of the *first* page directly after chapter one. This will be an "even" page. The "footers and headers" appears and your document becomes hazy.
2. Click on the blue-highlighted "link to previous" to unlink it.

3. Click on "different first page"
4. Click on "different odd and even pages"
5. Click on "Page Number" and choose where you want the number to be. I choose "bottom of page" and then I pick the option that shows the number on the far left for even pages.
6. Follow these same steps to add numbers to the odd pages only choosing the option that has the number on the far right.

Now you're ready to add the author name and title of your book in the headers.

1. Click on the left-hand top of the *first* page directly after chapter one. This will be an "even" page. The "footers and headers" appears and your document becomes hazy.
2. Click on the blue-highlighted "link to previous" to unlink it.
3. Click on "different first page"
4. Click on "different odd and even pages"
5. Click on "Header" and choose where you want the author name to be. I choose the option that has "blank three columns" the one that says "type here" three times, and then I delete the two I don't need. For the author name, I use the first "type here" and delete the middle and the one on the far right.

6. Follow these same steps to add the book title to the odd pages only choosing the option and then deleting the first two that say, "type here."

Most times this works like a charm, but sometimes it does not. However I have learned that giving up is never an option. Keep trying, and as with everything in life, practice makes perfect. I had a particularly difficult time putting page numbers in this book. Some of the issues I had were numbers repeating themselves within the same section or the wrong number on a page altogether. This is what I did to fix those problems.

1. Click on the corner of the page to **pull up headers and footers**. Now you can see how your sections are numbered. The front matter should all be lumped together in "section 1" and the first chapter should be "section 2."

2. I had an extra section before chapter one, making chapter one "section 3" which I didn't want. I changed that by **deleting the odd page break between the front matter that had divided the front matter into two sections.** To do this, enable the paragraph icon which looks like a backwards P in the HOME menu. It will allow you to see the inner formatting of your manuscript and will show you where and what kind of page break you have. I changed the "odd page break" to a simple "page break" and that merged the two sections into one. Now my first section has all my front matter and

"section 2" starts where it is supposed to—on chapter one.

3. Then I had to **delete all the incorrect page numbers** by going through one section at a time starting with section two. (Front matter shouldn't have page numbers or author name and title name in the headers and footers.) Using the "insert – page number – remove page number" didn't work for me this time, so I had to go through and delete each page number manually.

4. After getting rid of all page numbers, then I went through my manuscript **section by section and added the correct numbers.** Interestingly, I didn't have to add many of them manually, because I FIRST made sure that EACH section was unlinked to the previous section and EACH section had "different first page" clicked on. Once that was done, the numbers added themselves.

So, another problem that has cropped up from time to time with page numbering is that my sections were all starting on page one. I discovered that if I scrolled down through the pages, at the bottom of Word where it tells the pages and word count, though the numbers were true there, the sections were all starting over on page one – shown off to the right of the document while scrolling. Rather than experimenting with stripping everything out and starting over, I decided to figure out a way to make the page numbers still work. This is what I did.

Starting with the second section (chapter one), or the first section that has wrong numbers, these are the steps I followed after **clicking on the bottom or top corner of the document to open up headers and footers**.

1. Click on "unlink to previous."
2. Clear all numbers in troubled sections (say if the number repeats itself instead of moving forward in a sequential order.)
3. Go to "Page Number" – "Format Page Numbers."
4. Here's the super important part – each section needs to start on the appropriate page. So under "Format Page Numbers" make sure the fill-in box is set for **the page number of the first page in that section** (even though the first page will not show that number because you should have "Different First Page" already checked. All other pages in that section should now reflect that change.
5. I kept going back and forth between the document and the bottom blue strip of Word that tells the actual page number to check to see what the numbers were supposed to be in the document.
6. After the first page in the section's page number is entered under "Format Page Numbers", then you MUST NOT simply type in the number on the bottom of the page – you MUST pull down the menu that says "Page Numbers" and **use that to add numbers** in the appropriate place whether it is on the top or bottom, the left side or right side of the page. I put my even page numbers on the

bottom left hand side and my odd page numbers on the bottom right hand side.

Three

Images and Why You Don't Want Freebies

So, now we're to the fun part! For my images and background, I use Shutterstock, which cost $49.00 for five images that you will own the rights to use 250,000 times. I figure if my book sells enough to reach 250,000 times, then I can afford to rebuy the image again. I love Shutterstock because they are so versatile. You can find just the right picture for just the right mood for your fantastic cover.

First off, don't ever use a free image. What is free today may come back and bite you in the butt tomorrow. I had used several awesome images from Photobucket back in my pre-published days for my blogs, only to find out now that they are locking users out of their own blogs until they pay for images that are no longer free, even though *they had been free at the time of use*. Seems like a few lawsuits are in order here. Sure, changing your policy should effect the user from then on out, with *new images*, but not for prior use. Just remove the images, instead of locking people out where they can't even remove the images themselves. In fact, a better policy would be to start from where the user is, give them free reign over what they already have, and start charging for new images. I'll imagine they have lost thousands of potential customers with their poor policies. I know they've lost me.

Another freebie you might want to steer away from is Pixabay. I love Pixabay and use them often for school things, but I have yet to find an image that retains the vibrancy needed for a cover when enlarged. If you have, please let me know, and I will gladly update this. Okay, enough of my ranting.

Use good, reliable sources like Shutterstock. Shutterstock has never let me down, even when I downloaded two separate files that

I could not use with GIMP (vector.) They gave me credit for the files so I could then turn around and find a file I could use. Love them.

You can try out images from Shutterstock by simply clicking on them and saving them to a file. You can then manipulate it to your hearts content until you find the exact size and portion of the image you want to use. The image will retain the word Shutterstock stamped across it, but that way you can see if it will work for you first, and buy it later. You will be so amazed with how much more brilliant the image will be after you buy it too.

I speak from experience here. When I first started dabbling in creating my own covers, I didn't know I could try them out first.

So, now I own a few pictures that I've never used and may never use. Like this one that I thought would make a neat cover for my second book in the No Angel series where my main character is abducted and taken captive on a ship along with 100 other girls about to be auctioned off in a human trafficking scheme.

Originally, called Lip Reader, book three in the No Angel series, morphed into Destiny's Angel and has the perfect cover for the subject matter taken from the image above. The story line still involves the main character's abduction, but the backdrop of guardian angels and demons (sheydim) remain the silver thread that binds this epic story together.

You may go through all the steps and buy that perfect image, just to find out it isn't the perfect one after all.

For this book, *Fantastic Covers and How to Make Them*, I thought I had found the best cover image yet. I loved and purchased this image:

Isn't it fabulous? I thought it perfect in every way. But after creating the cover, I soon realized it wasn't quite the way I wanted it. I worked with it for hours, until I came up with this design:

I studied it for a long time before I realized that the image just wasn't cutting it. Up close, it loses its brilliance. While intriguing, it isn't sharp enough for me. Well, enough on choosing the right image—now go out there and find that perfect image!

Four

Fonts

If you use a special font, make sure you have the rights to it. Many font creators will allow you to use their fonts for personal use, but they will expect payment for their font if used in a book for sale.

Two of my favorite places to look for fonts are fontspace.com, and 1001fonts.com. I particularly like 1001fonts.com because you type in your title and each font shows you how it'll look instantly.

For example, I tried a font called, "Picture Font." I loved it but found it to be way too busy. You will want to earnestly consider the "busy-ness" of a font. An important thing to consider with book titles is readability. Can it be easily read if it were shown in a small thumbnail? If a potential reader cannot read your title, they are probably going to pass right by it.

Try different fonts out before you purchase them. To do this, download the file and install it. It might be different with your computer, but I have to restart my computer before the new font will show up in my established fonts. Remember, you haven't purchased the rights yet! I keep a list of purchased fonts and unpurchased fonts in a file as well as purchased and unpurchased Shutterstock images. I recommend doing this at the get-go. It makes it so much easier to find when needed. Also, on Shutterstock you can create files of images called "collections" for future use.

My fonts cost $35 to $40 and can be used for subsequent books. You'll want to have a few on hand as you create your cover, but if they still don't work for you, then be prepared to do a little more looking—there are thousands to choose from.

Five

Pause. Create. Repeat.

When Elias introduces his best friend Jaron to his magical world of fairies, wizards, and castles, will he ever want to return to the dull world of school and homework, especially after meeting Elieli, the fairy princess of Estraelia? And will Elias have to alter his memory, or will Jaron be able to keep the secret that Elias Rey, a sophomore at PVHS, is a wizard, and the youngest heir of Elderberry?

The Wood Fairies of Estraelia is book two in the Sons of Elderberry series, and it was one of my favorite covers to create.

I started with an image of a beautiful fairy, but she was dressed rather skimpily as you can see in this picture. So, I set about teaching myself how to clothe her by watching YouTube videos, pausing them, adjusting the image, going back to the video, and then repeating. I covered most of her bare skin by adding a green jumpsuit. Through watching YouTube videos, I learned how to shade her jumpsuit and make pearl accents, and then voila! —a fully clothed, modest fairy to meet all reading ages.

If you look closely at the cover, you can see three smaller fairies. They were not part of the original image. I purchased the rights to them on Shutterstock, removed their backgrounds, and adjusted their clothing as well.

For instance, in the original image, this fairy was tapping pixie dust on a bird in a cage.

Using GIMP, I erased everything but the fairy and her wand, reduced her size down, and placed her on my cover positioning her pixie dust falling on the larger fairy's flower.

I did the same thing with the two smaller fairies. First, I removed them from their original backgrounds.

Then I copied part of their existing clothing and pulled the newly created image down over their bottoms.

The leafy frame surrounding my cover was created by isolating existing leaves and then manipulating them around the edges. Sounds like a lot of work, and it was, but I absolutely love doing it!

Remember to always purchase the right to your images and fonts. I purchased the rights to the four images through Shutterstock for about $40.00 and the font for $35.00.

I did the same thing with all of my covers, purchased the images and fonts, and then set about manipulating them by watching YouTube videos, pausing, and repeating. This is book one in the No Angel series.

With the cover for *Angel with an Attitude*, I purchased the rights to the font, the wings, the scroll effect I added to the font and wings, the guardian angel, and the dark blue sky. I was careful with the images I chose always striving for the overall effect I was seeking. The entire cover is so Jonathan Stewart, the main character in *Angel with an Attitude*. He didn't like earth and doesn't want to return, but he has to, because it's required by all post-mortal spirits to go back to earth as a guardian angel at least once.

There are five books in the *No Angel* series with more to come. *Earthbound Angel* is book two. *Earthbound Angel's* backdrop is heaven—or the premortal world we came from before being born to earth.

Destiny's Angel is book three. We find Angie, previously known as Sophie in the premortal world in book two, abducted and taken aboard a ship, along with dozens of other young women, about to be auctioned off to the highest bidder.

Earth Angel is book four, where because of his hilarious antics, Jonathan receives a rather interesting assignment on earth. And book five, *Harold Angel Sing*, is my all-time most favorite book to write and deals with special-needs children on earth.

The entire No Angel series carries the escapades of Jonathan throughout, with the subplots of several other premortal spirits born to earth, living amongst the ever-constant backdrop of the spirit world.

My purpose in writing the *No Angel* series was to introduce the concept of a very real spirit world that surrounds us and the busy things that happen in our behalf, both for us (guardian angels), and against us (demons.)

I once had a reader ask me, "how do you know about these things?" It's because I write from the many paranormal experiences I've had from a young age up to adulthood. If you want to know more, read, "Facing Mortality; Dreams and Other Significant Things."

With all of my *No Angel* covers, I kept the title font and series font the same. That helps the reader to easily identify your series. I purchased the rights to different skies as the background and a variety of statues of angels. You can check out more of my covers by going to my website at www.theresasneed.com.

Six

Steps to Creating a Fantastic Cover

Follow me while I create a cover from scratch.

First

You should have a general idea of what you want your book cover to say. Make it match your genre and story. Choose images that best express your awesome story. Download two or three previews of images first—try them out on your cover before buying them.

For this book, originally called, *Cover Design*, I perused several images. I thought, "What best will show the excitement of making my cover come to life?" And then I reasoned, "My cover come to life, with a generic title like, *"Cover Design?"* I didn't think so. But how about *Fantastic Covers and How to Make Them.* I liked the title immediately and the possibility of injecting pure fantasy into my cover began to form in my mind. The search was on.

I went to Shutterstock and began looking through images I thought would best represent my topic—fantastic covers. The four images I considered are below:

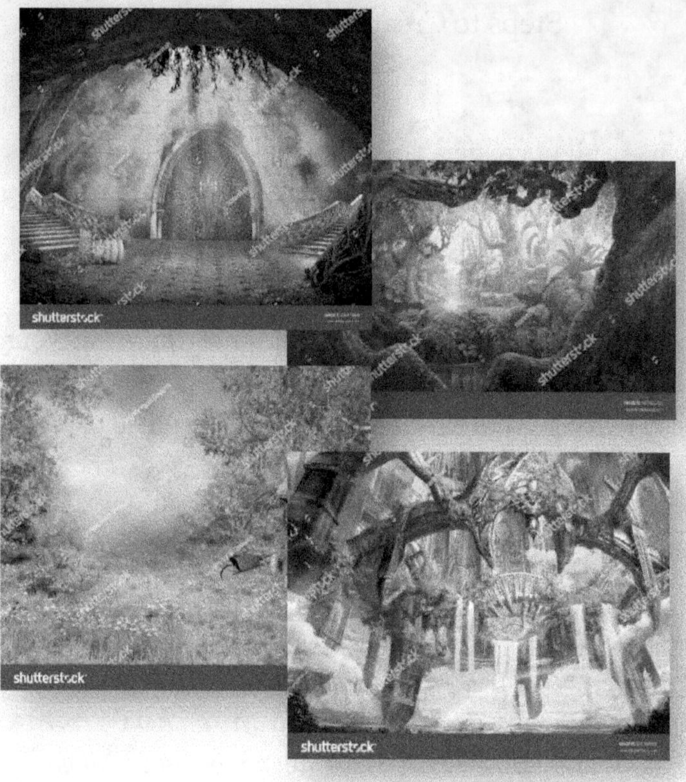

I downloaded them as previews and tried each one of them out. I chose the last one and created this cover:

But as I mentioned before, for some reason, this cover wasn't right. I thought, "Why isn't it working? Maybe the image in the background needs to be smaller to capture more of the fantasy effect." So I resized it and came up with this:

Still, not happy, I took it one step further. I thought, "What if I resize the image once more? What if I made it even smaller? This is what I came up with:

I was able to capture more fantasy with the smaller image, but it was still not there. I went back to Shutterstock and found another image. I did not purchase the image, but downloaded a preview of it. Here's what it looked like after replacing the image under the titles.

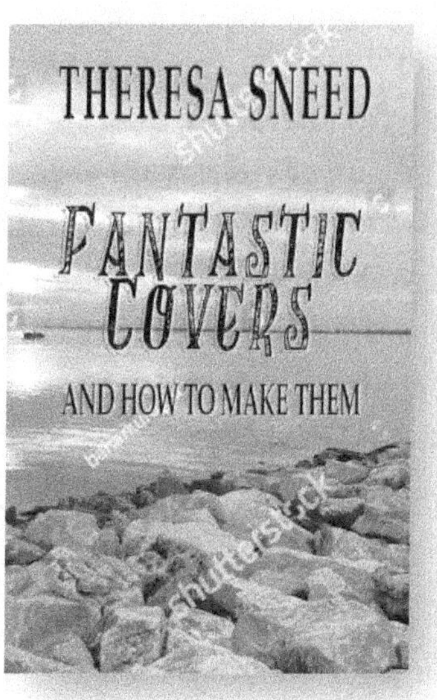

I don't know why I like it better. There is absolutely no fantasy in this image, but after studying it for a while, and deciding it was good, I went ahead and purchased it. And now, I am going to walk you through the steps I took to create this cover as I do it.

Second

So, you've downloaded your images into a file which you named Shutterstock Unpurchased Images or something like that. It doesn't matter what you name it, as long as you can find it when needed. You've downloaded GIMP for free and you're ready to use it. You've signed into a free account with KDP. Now I'm going to walk you through creating your cover from the beginning.

You either know how long your book is or approximately how long, not in regular 8x11 format, but in book format as explained in chapter two. This is important, because the spine on your book needs to be set to the correct width. *Fantastic Covers and How to Create Them* is approximately 75 pages. So, after signing on to KDP, I went to the search bar in the upper right-hand corner and typed in "book cover templates." On the left hand side midway down it says, "Configure your Template" and then "Interior Type, Trim Size, Number of Pages, Paper Color" and then "Build Template." Fill in each section and then click, Build Template.

Another page comes up that says, "Download your Template, Click here to begin Download, 200kb Compressed Zip File and What's in the Zip," where it shows you a PDF file—that's the one you'll want, but you won't get it until you click download. A screen comes up with an icon that says, "Extract All." Click on it. Then you'll be prompted to select a destination and a folder. Off to the right, it says, "browse." Click browse and now you have the option to select a folder to download into. I recommend creating a new folder. The option to create a new folder should be on the page you are on. Create the folder and name it something like, "Book Templates," which is where you will drop book templates for new books as needed. Select your new folder named Book Templates and then you'll see that the download has put that as its destination. Download the book template file, and now you'll see it come up in that file, and you'll be able to find it when needed.

Minimize the file by clicking on the two "pages" in the upper right hand corner of the screen. It should now be small but not completely disappear from the screen. Any opened files need to be minimized completely down until the desktop remains so that just the desktop and the book template screen are showing.

Now, click on the file. Mine says, 5.5x8.5_BW_80. The PNG file and the PDF file comes up. I use PDF. I'm sure there is a better way of doing this, but what I do is drag the PDF file to my desktop. That's why I minimized all the files and cleared the way to my desktop.

You should be able to see the file on your desktop. Now open GIMP and minimize it. It won't go down much, but enough for you to grab it with your cursor and pull it to where you can see the book template on your desktop. Now, click and drag the book template inside GIMP, then click "Import." There you have it—your template is now ready to use to create your fantastic cover.

Third

Before you drop your image into the template, pull lines from the top and the left side to the dotted lines that delineate the cover and spine of your book. They are shown on your template as the lighter inside lines in the template.

To do this, take your cursor and touch the top of the GIMP screen where the number line is and then click and hold down to drag a line to the top lighter line of your book. Then go back up to the top of the screen again and pull another line way down to the bottom lighter line of your cover. Do the same thing for the side lines, pulling four lines over to cover the outside edges of the book and the inside edges of the spine. This will help you to see exactly what will show on you cover and spine.

Fourth

Now you will add your image. In GIMP, click on "File" and then "Open as Layers." Find the file you put your image in and click on it. Your image should appear and cover the whole book cover template. Like this:

My image above doesn't show the lines because they are only visible on GIMP. You may not be happy with it, or you may want to isolate a part of it for the front cover. I like mine just the way it is, but if I wanted to, I could click on the newly created file on the right hand side of GIMP.

It should show two things, the book template with an open eye to the left of it and the stock-photo file of the image you just dropped into GIMP with an open eye to the left of it. Anything you create on your cover will show up in this elongated file on the right of GIMP. If you want to alter the image, then first you have to click and highlight the stock-photo with an open eye. That tells GIMP you are about to manipulate that file in some way.

Before we go any further, make sure you save your work. When you save it, look closely to where it will put it, and change its destination to a "new file", which you will call the name of your book. Remember to save your work often.

56

Moving on, to move the image, highlight it in the elongated file to the right, then choose the Move Tool to move it around. On the left hand side of the screen in GIMP there are several tools. The "Move Tool" is the two lines crossing each other. You can check out each tool by holding your cursor over it. It will tell you its name. Click on the "Move Tool" and move your cursor over to your image. You should see a small icon of the Move Tool move with your cursor. Once you click and hold down your cursor, the image will move with you to where you want it, and the lines you created will help you to see certain parts of the image in different locations on the front cover.

You'll want to make sure that you're using your image to its best ability. After downloading it, if you saw the outline of the actual image over the book template as dotted lines and blank space, it means that part of your image is not showing on your cover.

I recommend reducing you image down to fit your cover. To do this, click on the "Scale Tool" and then on the image. A grid pops up over the image. To the left a "scale" box pops up where it tells you the height and width of the image. To the left of the height and width there is a broken chain link. Click on that link and lock it first to retain the proportions of your image. Now when you reduce it down, the entire image will reduce down together.

Start by reducing the height, and the width will automatically adjust itself. Reduce it down as far as you'd like. If you go too far, it'll disappear off the page. If it does, just click "ctrl z" to return to the previous step. Then go over to the tools and click on the "Move Tool." Making sure that the stock-photo is still highlighted, bring the Move Tool over to it. Click and drag the image to where you want it. Continue to resize and move your image until it fits your cover.

Let's say you like the image in a place where it now leaves the back cover empty or partially empty. Easy to fix. First pull the image to where you want it. Then you can do one of two things. You can create a new layer with a solid color for your back cover, or you can duplicate the stock-photo by right-clicking on it and selecting, "Duplicate Layer." You will not see it, because it is directly over the first image. Highlight the new image that appeared in the elongated file to the right, take the Move Tool, and move the duplicated image to where you want it.

Make sure the first image is above the duplicated one, or vice versa. In the elongated file, click on the stock photo and drag it above or beneath its duplicate. If you click the eye off, you can better see which one you were moving.

Here, I duplicated the image and then flipped the duplicated image with the "Flip Tool" and then I dragged the flipped image to the exact point of where the two are the same.

You can see that by moving the image to the right, I now have more color on the front cover. I actually think I might like that but won't know until I add the titles.

Fifth

To add titles, click on the "Text Tool." It is a capital A. Bring it over to the front cover and click. A text box comes up. As soon as you start typing, you can see a new file pop up over to the right in the elongated file. For ease, above that file, at the very top, click on the small arrow and move the file over until you come to "Text." Here you can change the size and font of the text. The font I used for my cover is called, VTKS RECOVER MB1. I will purchase it if I decide to use it in the end. So, as you wrote the title, you couldn't see it on your cover? That means it is below the stock-photo. Press on the left arrow at the top over the Text file until it comes back to the file with your image, duplicated image, the Text file with your title, and the book template icon.

Highlight the Text file with your title and drag it above the stock-photo image on your front cover. Now you can see your title and adjust the font and size to your needs by going back to the Text file to the right. If you can't find that Text file, you may have to click on the "A" called the "Text Tool" and then on the title on your front cover. Now use the arrows above the elongated file to the right to find the Text file.

Use the "Move Tool" to move your title around to where you want it. Don't forget to highlight the Text file with your title in the elongated file first. If you don't, you'll move whatever you were working on last. Remember, to fix this, simply click on "ctrl z" to return to the previous step.

For subtitle, do the same thing. Click on the Text Tool, A, and then on the front cover, where you want the subtitle to be. Follow the same steps above to either change your font or its size. I did both, but I also stretched the text with the Scale Tool. I found I had to edit the subtitle and started over with the original size, went to the text file and adjusted the letter spacing to "2" and then used the Scale Tool to stretch the text, and the Move Tool to move the subtitle to the perfect location.

But then I discovered that the tiny boat on the front cover was blocked by the title. I first tried to move the image to unblock the ship, but it wasn't big enough and didn't cover the whole front cover, so I used the Scale Tool and increased the size of the image. Then I deleted the old duplicate image as it was now the wrong size, made a duplicate of the newly-sized image, and then flipped it. I pulled it to the end of the newly created image so that the edges match nicely. Of course, I'm going to have to do this again when I purchase the new image, but I wanted you to see all the steps. And who knows? Maybe after I am finished, I won't like this as well and may not purchase the image. Here is what it looks like so far:

Now, I will add the author name by following the same steps I used to create the title and subtitle. I used one of my favorite generic fonts for the subtitle, called Book Antiqua Bold, and I will use it for the author name too. It's a nice, bold font. I use capital letters for my subtitle and author name, and I adjust the letter spacing to two as well, then stretch the text with the scale tool. Then I move the author name to where I want it with the Move Tool.

By the way, when you are moving the Move Tool over your front cover, if you see a hand along with it, it means it hasn't located the file you highlighted yet, and it will move the wrong file, probably the image under it. Just keep moving the Move Tool icon around slowly until the hand disappears and then click on the correct image to move it.

I've added my author name now and this is what it looks like. Now I will add depth to my titles.

First, I clicked on the title I wanted to enhance. I did my author name first by highlighting it in the elongated file to the right. Then I clicked on Filters, Light and Shadow, and then Drop Shadow in the menu bar on the top of the screen. An image of GIMP popped up on the bottom of my screen and flashed yellow. I clicked on that and then adjusted the offset x to 2, the offset y to 2, the blur radius to 4, the color to black, and the opacity to 90 with resizing checked. Something didn't look right, so I enlarged the entire book file to 100%, by clicking on the 100% icon on the bottom of the GIMP screen. I will change that back, after I look at the author title.

I didn't like it, because I had forgotten to change the color to a different color than my text. So, I clicked on "ctrl z" and went back to the previous step, then readjusted the color. I wanted it to blend in with the image, so I pulled the color from the image.

To do that, I highlighted the stock-photo image, chose the Color Picker Tool, and ran it over the stock-photo image until I found the perfect accent color. When you choose a color, the color changes in the Foreground and Background color box. Keep doing it until you find the perfect color. When you click on the new color in the Foreground and Background color box, a menu will pop up and tell you the color code—a series of numbers and lower case letters in the HTML notation menu.

Now when you go back to Filters, you can adjust the color using the color code. Remember to highlight the title, as you were just on the stock-photo image, and are now are back to the title again.

I didn't like the blur radius this time, so I clicked on "ctrl z" and then adjusted the blur radius to 2. It looks a lot better. I used those same settings for my title and my subtitle. Highlighting them one at a time, all I had to do was go to Filters and then choose Repeat Drop Shadow. It was that simple.

My front cover could've been complete, but after looking at the arrangement of my title with my author name, I decided to move them around to see if they might look better in different locations. First I locked the drop shadow to the title before moving it, and then unlocked it before locking the author name with its drop shadow. I could've merged them together, but then if I wanted to change them later, I'd have to redo the files. Locking them together is easier.

To lock them, click on the empty box in between the eye and the title, and the eye and the drop shadow beneath it. Now they will move together. Use the Move Tool to move them to a different location. Then unlock them and lock the author name the same way. However, as of 2024, the newest version of Gimp immediately locks the drop shadows to the fonts after you create the drop shadow, so that last part will not be necessary unless you have the older version of Gimp, (I'd upgrade if you do.) The mage below shows the fonts with the added drop shadows.

The back cover blurb is next. Click on the Text Tool and place it on the back cover. You'll need to adjust the text color back to black, unless your cover is really dark and a lighter color works best. First pull some lines over to use as guidelines for your text. Then click on the text on the back cover and using the Move Tool, position it within those guidelines. Now adjust the text position. I used the justified choice in the justify menu in the Text Box. It's a small icon alongside three other choices. And then, I readjusted the length of the text in the text box to the guidelines.

I decided to center my first line of text to make it pop out, so I changed the justification to center and increased the size of the text. Then I stretched the text and repeated the drop shadow for a greater effect. Now I'll move on the back cover blurb.

Oops! I forgot to tell you something about creating back cover blurbs. Before you start typing, place the cursor over the sides of the text box and pull it over and down, or the whole text will stretch out in one single long line. If that happens, reduce the entire book file down, locate the edge of the text, and pull it back to the back cover blurb. You'll need to adjust the color and justification too, if it's still on center.

The repeated drop shadow didn't work for my back cover blurb. I fixed it by clicking on "ctrl z" and then I readjusted it. The text size was too large, so I deleted the drop shadow, resized the text, and then reused the repeat drop shadow. Then after locking the back cover blurb and its drop shadow together, I used the Move Tool to

reposition the text a bit higher. You can see in the image below, that the cover is coming together.

Sixth

Now, I'm going to show you how to put your name, your title, and if it's a series, the series number on the spine. With a short book like this one, you will not be able to have a name and title on the spine, but if you book is thicker, you will need one. I will show you the steps, but then delete it from my file, as from experience, I know that KDP will come back and tell you to remove it due to the thin spine.

First, make a duplicate of both the title of your book and its drop shadow. In the elongated file to the right, drag one of the drop shadows up to one of the titles. The drop shadow needs to be directly beneath the image it is attached to. Then lock the duplicated title of your book with its duplicated drop shadow and use the Move Tool to move off of the original title on your cover. Just move it aside so you can see it while adjusting.

Next, click on the Scale Tool. Then click on the duplicated title with the eye to highlight it and then click on duplicated title on your front cover. Using the Scale Tool, reduce it down to fit in your spine. In my case, I had to create another title because my title had two lines and would need to be side by side on the spine.

Then using the Rotate Tool, click on the newly created title and spin it around as close to 90% as you can. Using the Move Tool, move your title to the spine. Repeat these steps with your author name and series number.

I liked this cover, so I purchased the image. Now all I have to do is download into this file. I won't need to change any of the text only the background images. First, I clicked off the eye beside the stock-photo and its duplicate. Then I went back to Shutterstock and bought the image saving it in my "Shutterstock Purchased Images" folder.

Then click on "File, Open as Layers" in the menu bar in the upper right hand side of GIMP. Search for your "Shutterstock Paid Images" find the new file which will not say "stock-photo" but will have a number beside it. Click on it. You can now see how much more brilliant your image is.

Click on the new image in the elongated bar to the right and pull it down below all of you text so you can see them. The image is much larger than after I adjusted it. I could've kept it, but decided to play with it with my text in place. What I discovered thrilled me! The larger image when repositioned was perfect. I didn't even have to create a duplicate image to fix the back. I did lock the title and drop shadow together and move them up a bit and then the subtitle and its drop shadow.

I'm ready now to cut the front cover out of the full cover. Before you do that, save your file in a different name. I always keep it the way it is but add "front cover" to the name. That way you will have two files. You will need a full cover with back cover blurb for your novel, and a separate front cover for eBooks and advertising. Here is the final result of my full cover.

To make the front cover, first save your file a second time, and then using the Crop Tool, position it in the upper right-hand corner of your front cover where the inside dotted lines cross. Where the lines cross, put the hollow x so that the lines are inside it. Click and drag down to the far left corner. Release. Then click on the box right beside that far left corner.

Now you have a front cover. On mine, my name was a bit off center, so I highlighted my author name, locked the name with its drop shadow, used the Move Tool, and moved it slightly to the left. I went back and adjusted my full cover too. It's easier to do if you click the eye next to the purchased image off and then the eye next to the book template off, because then you can count the squares on each side of your text and make them an even number. When adjusting the title and the subtitle, I locked all four of them together and moved them at the same time. It helps also to remove the guidelines by going to View in the top menu and clicking off the checkmark beside guides. Well, what do you think?

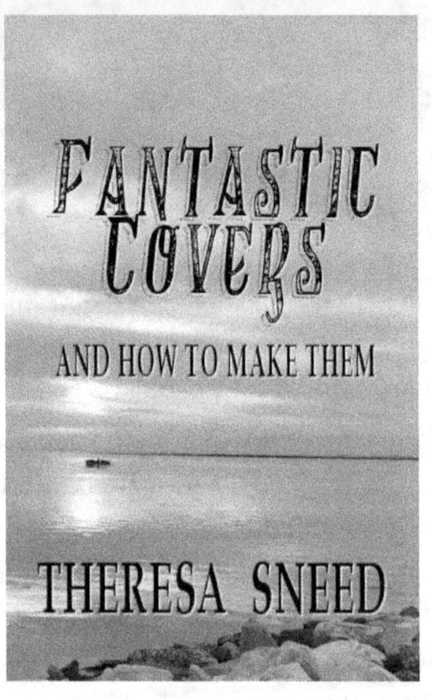

I hope this small book will help you on your way to creating your own covers. I don't believe in luck so best of blessings to you!

Author Theresa Sneed graduated cum laude with a BA in education. Though retired as a fulltime teacher, she enjoys visiting classrooms and sharing her writing journey. Her books are unique; each story takes you places you've never imagined before. She writes across six genres: mystery and suspense, fantasy, historical fiction/time-travel, realistic paranormal, nonfiction motivational, and children's books. All of Theresa's fiction books have elements of sweet romance, and while none of her books have profanity or sexually explicit scenes, each book is intriguing and white-knuckle intense—the kind you can't put down.

Her nonfiction books are *So You Want to Write: A Guide to Writing Your First Book* where Theresa has pulled together her fifteen steps to writing success; *Fantastic Covers and How to Make Them*; and *Facing Mortality: Dreams & Other Significant Things* a compilation of Theresa's paranormal experiences that drove her to write her *No Angel* series and many scenes in her other works.

Theresa's first picture book explores the woes of sibling tattletales. *Brown Nose Bear* is a children's story that kept her own children and now her grandchildren giggling and rethinking whether tattletales should or should not be told.

The *No Angel* series is the story about a guardian angel with an attitude, and the ever present, but misunderstood spirit world. There are five published books in the series with many more to come. Book one, formerly called *No Angel*, is now called *Angel with an Attitude*; book two, formerly called *Earthbound*, is now called *Earthbound Angel*; book three is called *Destiny's Angel*; book four is called *Earth Angel*, and book five is called *Harold Angel Sing*.

With the addition of *Missing Medallion*, The *Sons of Elderberry* series has three books, books one and two called *Elias of Elderberry* and *The Wood Fairies of Estraelia*. Harry-Potterish with wizards, fairies, elves, pixies, yōkai shapeshifters, and dragons, this story has it all! Theresa anticipates another book or two to finish this series.

Escape is the story of a fifteen-year-old girl abducted by a corrupt sheriff in the 70's. He keeps her captive in his cellar for five years, until she escapes with his truck and his young daughter. *Escape* is book one in the *Escape* series. Book two is *You Can't Hide*, and book three, *Find Her Keep Her,* ends the gripping saga.

As the ninth great-granddaughter of one of the women hanged as a witch in Salem, Theresa Sneed has a vested interest in telling her story as accurately as possible. She wrote the *Salem Witch Haunt* series to be a voice for her grandmother. Thoroughly researched, all interactions with real people from that era are based on primary sources. In book one, *Salem Witch Haunt*, the trial scene with Theresa's 9th great-grandmother, Susannah Martin is taken from Reverend Samuel Parris's handwritten transcript verbatim. *Salem Witch Haunt* was intended to be a standalone book, until the shocking ending made it apparent that the characters were not finished telling their story. Hence, *Return to Salem*, where the second set of trials and hangings in Salem, 1692, are masterfully woven into the story. *Salem Bewitched* completes this series with the last of the trials and hangings and the peine forte et dure of Giles Corey. Added to this series comes, *Salem Witch Haunt: Stranger Than Fiction,* where footnotes pointing to the primary sources embedded in the series have been added as a companion to this incredible historical fiction. Both *Return to Salem: Stranger Than*

Fiction and *Salem Bewitched: Stranger Than Fiction* will come later.

Learn more about Theresa's books at www.theresasneed.com. She loves hearing from her readers and may be contacted through her website or through her email at tmsneed@theresasneed.com Stay connected with new releases and free eBook offers by signing up at her website.